BEGINNINGS

by CAROL LYNN PEARSON

Illustrated by Trevor Southey

Doubleday & Company, Inc.
Garden City, New York
1975

ISBN: 0-385-07711-4
Library of Congress Catalog Card Number 74-028894
Copyright © 1967 by Carol Lynn Pearson
All Rights Reserved
Printed in the United States of America

PREFACE

*And when he was entered into a ship . . .
there arose a great tempest . . . And his dis-
ciples came to him, and awoke him, saying,
Lord, save us: we perish. And he saith unto
them, Why are ye fearful, O ye of little faith?
Then he arose, and rebuked the winds and the
sea; and there was a great calm.*
(St. Matthew 8:23-26)

There are so many storms in life. It is often difficult to
find solutions to our problems. Some of us despair. Others
seek an escape. Those who follow these paths, however, have
never fully realized that life was meant to be a challenge
and an opportunity.

The challenge lies in being able to choose between dif-
ferent types of satisfactions. Wisdom lies in being able to
choose the diamond instead of its glass imitation.

The opportunity consists in learning from one's ex-
perience.

*If thou art called to pass through tribulation
. . . if fierce winds become thine enemy; if the
heavens gather blackness, and all the elements
combine to hedge up the way . . . know thou, my
son, that all these things shall give thee ex-
perience, and shall be for thy good. The Son
of Man hath descended below them all. Art thou
greater than he?*
(Doctrine and Covenants 122:6-8)

Among the great Gifts He offers to us are the Principles
which He knew must be understood, accepted and lived if
we are to attain the destiny forseen for each of us from the
Beginning of Beginnings.

*Behold, I am Jesus Christ . . . In me shall all
mankind have light, and that eternally, even
they who believe on my name; and they shall
become my sons and my daughters.*
(Ether 3:14)

Carol Lynn understands these Principles. In humility
and with integrity she has explored Their deep and delicate
meanings.

All of us who read her poems (and may there be many
of us) can best express our gratitude to Him and to her by
seeking with all our hearts and souls to "become" His Son
or Daughter. Then we will find Peace and Joy as He under-
stood them. We can sleep when the wind blows.

Reed H. Bradford

CONTENTS

BEGINNINGS

Today
You came running
With a small specked egg
Warm in your hand.
You could barely understand,
I know,
As I told you
Of Beginnings —
Of egg and bird
Told, too,
That years ago
You began,
Smaller than sight.
And then,
As egg yearns for sky
And seed
Stretches to tree,
You became —
Like me.

Oh,
But there's
So much more.
You and I,
Child,
Have just begun.

Think:
Worlds from now
What might we be? —
We,
Who are seed
Of Diety.

ANALYSIS

I am,
They announce
Authoritatively,
A product of
Environment
And heredity.

True.
But my substance
Is laced with
One thing more:
Thin threads of
The now-forgotten
Everything
That I was
Before.

RITUAL

Why ritual?
May I not receive
Christ without burial
By water?
If I remember
That He bled,
If I believe,
What need for
Sacramental bread?

Only this I know:
All cries out
For form —
No impulse
Can rest
Until somehow
It is manifest.
Even my spirit,
Housed in heaven,
Was not content
Until it won
Embodiment.

OF THE MYSTERIES

I know only as much of God and the world
As a creature with two eyes must;
But what I do understand I love,
And what I don't understand, I trust.

THE ELEVENTH HOUR

Had I been born
To other centuries —
How pleasant
To stretch
In the sun
And choose from
All life's
Possibilities
This one,
Or that.
To prove the
Earth is round,
Or tame the ocean,
To write a dictionary,
Or expound
On Shakespeare's
Subtle irony.

But these are
Daytime jobs.
And,
As I was born
To time's
Saturday night,
My ordained task
Is to kindle
The Sabbath light.

FROM A WRITER
OF PLEASANT THINGS

You must forgive
This tendency of mine
To believe
The world holds
Something good,
Something fine.

The habit
Has troubled me
From childhood —
When I even
Preferred to
Build a snowman
Than to take
A romp through
The garbage can.

THE LORD SPEAKS TO A
LITERARY DEBAUCHÉ
NEWLY ARRIVED IN HEAVEN

Impressive indeed, this shelf of books
On which all the earth-critics dote.
But oh, my son, how I wish that you
Had read the book I wrote.

MILK BEFORE MEAT

Why worry on
Exactly how
A body will arise
Once a man dies?

I can't even
Understand
The manifest things —
Like how
A seagull flies
From merely
Having wings.

PERSPECTIVE FROM MORTALITY

My life is patterned as the palm
Of a rain-washed leaf, calm,
Cut, and full.
But
I view my life from underneath,
Which — like the patterned leaf —
Is fuzzed and dull.

A NEW DIMENSION TO FAITH

When some new pain pierces my life
Rebellion begins to cry,
"God knew this would come and He approved!"
But wait, long ago—so did I.

KEEPING THE BUCK

I can't blame God for what I am,
Nor for the troubles that surround me:
He did His best with what I was
When He found me.

THE PLAN

An unseemly design for ascension,
That with a cross and a crown of briar
We should lift Christ toward heaven
So that He could lift us higher.

TO A BELOVED SKEPTIC

I cannot talk with you of God
Since sober wise you grew;
So my one recourse in charity
Is to talk with God of you.

THE LESSON

Yes, my fretting,
Frowning child,
I could cross
The room to you
More easily.
But I've already
Learned to walk,
So I make you
Come to me.

Let go now —
There!
You see?

Oh, remember
This simple lesson,
Child,
And when
In later years
You cry out
With tight fists
And tears —
"Oh, help me,
God — please." —
Just listen
And you'll hear
A silent voice:

"I would, child,
I would.
But it's you,
Not I,
Who needs to try
Godhood."

NATIVITY SCENE

Touch the tiny Jesus gently now —
Put him in the bed.
No, dear, I don't know why the wise man
Wears a turban on his head.
That's just the way they dressed.
Be careful with the lamb—it's best
To hold him with both hands.
It's late in Bethlehem —
That's why the star shines bright.
It showed the wise men where to come.

No, dear, the star can't really shine.
It's wood—it's just pretend.
But last night,
The star we wished on high above the moon —
That was real. Remember?

The lamb won't bleat, dear.
Even when you're asleep.
It's a sort of clay. But you did hear
Your uncle's sheep
Calling in alarm
Through the midnight of a snow-filled farm.

The baby Jesus?
Clay.
But listen, dear (put down the lamb) —
I've a promise for you,
A promise God will keep:
As you've seen stars
And as you've heard the sheep,
One day you'll know and hear and see
This Jesus too,
In reality.

THE BENEFICIARY

I was not there.
But they say
It happened for me.
On the cross it happened,
And in the tomb.
For me —
Vicariously.

But how?
It was His sacrifice
Not mine.
It was He who wept,
Who bled,
Not me.

Except —
Why, look —
At the flick of a finger
I instantly receive
What Edison
Gave his full life
To achieve.

Perhaps,
If one man,
Searching the skies,
Willed us the key
To conquer night —
May not another,
A greater,
Bequeath from the cross
The key to
Eternal light?

THOUGHTS
IN THE CHAPEL

How I will
Greet the Lord
In heaven
I do not know.

But here
With the
Sabbath organ
And water and bread,
Or at home
Beside my bed —
Whenever we converse,
Just Him and me
(Watching the sunset
Or the sea),
I can at least
Rehearse.

TO ONE WHO WORRIES
ABOUT BEING FOUND

Does the flower fret
That the bee
Might forget
To buzz by?

Ah, no.
One concern
Has she,
And she tends
It well:
Her own smell.

THE EMBRYO

Love is no eagle,
Strong amid
The heights.
It is an egg —
A fertile,
Fragile
Possibility.
Hold it warm
Within your wing,
Beneath your breast.

Perhaps in heaven
Love can live
Self-nourished,
Free.
But in this world,
Where mountains fall
And east winds blow,
Oh, careful —
Love is embryo.

MY SEASON

Seeing the tree
Beneath a baptism of snow,
You may call her barren.
But is it so?
And for all your watchings
On a March night
When the twigs seem dark
And the bark
Feels cold to your hand —
Can you call her fruitless
And so leave?

She smiles,
Calm in the station
Of seasons
And in the ordination
Of sun, and sap, and spring.

As for me?
You turn away,
Impatient with
The promises you've seen.
But—inside I fill
And pulse and flow
With the urgency of green.

I've a season,
Like the tree.
And all your
Faithless doubts
Will not destroy
The rising spring
In me.

ANOTHER BIRTH

I did not bring
The anticipation
Of birth —
Of forging my spirit
With flesh.

As the moment
Neared,
I think
I held my breath
(If spirits breathe)
And made a
Reverent plunge
Into embodiment,
Mortality.

Yes —
Even unremembering
I know the
Wonderment,
The awe.
For I stand staring
At another birth
That swells my heart
With the hugeness
Of beginnings.
In a moment
I am born as wife —
Given another body
And another life.

AT THE ALTAR

The thought
Of forever
Teased my mind
Like a mountain
Through a thickly
Misted view.

But today the
Veil dissolved
To show —
Eternity
Is you.

A JUDGMENT

I have been judged.
Already, mortal,
I have stood
At heaven's bar
While my soul
Was read aloud.
And —
Oh, listen —
Not proud,
But too full
For silence
I sing the decree.
God smiled at me
(And all of
Heaven did too),
Smiled as He gave
A sentence
Toward salvation —
Gave me you.

THE REASON

A certain panic
Finds me
When I see
A forest, a train,
A library.
So many trees to touch,
Places,
Faces yet to view,
And, too,
So many words to read.

If I concede
All space to earth,
All time to life,
The disproportion
Is absurd
(My tiny taste
And the giant waste
Of all creation
I've not known).
What a wretched,
Faithless view
Of God's economy.

It isn't true.
The forest, the train,
The library —
Are why we have
Eternity.

PRAYER AT TABLE

The food, yes —
But most of all
Bless
Me.
The bread is
Full and good,
As I would be.
Oh, Lord,
My only leaven,
Work —
Warm me —
Let me lift
Toward heaven.

GUILT

I have no vulture sins, God,
That overhang my sky,
To climb, grey-feathering the air,
And swoop carnivorously.

It's just the tiny sins, God,
That from memory appear
Like tedious, buzzing flies to dart
Like static through my prayer.

AUTHORITY

There is
A fire that filters
Down the night
Of this world—
A light-line
Sparked by God
In human lanterns.
I watch them
And my way clears.

But here
One flickers,
Then fails,
And farther off
Another's glow
Guides only the
Largest steps.

Still I can see.
For God also kindled
(And gently blows
To brighten)
A flame
In me.

PURIFICATION

If the sea
And the sun
Can bleach a bone
Til it's whiter
Than a gull,
Cleaner than foam —

Oh, how bright
My soul
Can emerge,
Purged
On the beach
Of Christ's water
And light.

And —

How calm
And warm
His sand.

THE FORGIVING

Forgive?
Will I forgive,
You cry.
But
What is the gift,
The favor?

You would lift
Me from
My poor place
To stand beside
The Savior.
You would have
Me see with
His eyes,
Smile,
And with Him
Reach out to
Salve
A sorrowing heart —
For one small
Moment
To share in
Christ's great art.

Will I forgive,
You cry.
Oh,
May I —
May I?

PROPERTY

Collect property?
The road to the
New Jerusalem
Will seem hard
To those with
A fortune
To discard.

Just one lovely thing
That I may
Reverently bear
To the City of God
(A silver plate
Or perhaps a ring) —
This,
With the greater
Wealth locked lightly
In my breast,
Is all the estate
I care
To accumulate.

THE TITHE

Into the crockery
Of a crumbling earth
I pour my
Nine-tenth's wealth.
But how the
Remaining coin
Cheers my economy,
As it clinks
In the golden cup
Of eternity.

THE MEASURE

Friend,
Do you measure land
With a barometer?
Can you understand
The law of gravity
By testing
The freezing point of mud
At its greatest density?

There is no God
By knowledge's rules?
Friend,
Examine your tools.

To discover God
You must form your plan
To the nature
Of God Himself,
Not the nature of man.
The only key
Is that forgotten faculty
That pulses through you
Now and then,
Eluding the hand
And startling the mind.
Spirit, it's called.

Friend,
You will not find
God through mistaken tools.
Who weighs a stone
With a measuring tape?
Fools.

PRAYER

This radio set
Called prayer
Is designed
For remarkably
Simple repair.
When the lines fail,
There is no doubt
Which half
Of the set
Is out.

THE OFFERING

For ancient wrongs
God required
The burning of flesh,
An offering fresh
From the flocks.

But Christ turned
The outside in.
And for my sin
God demands
The harder part:
No yearling lamb
On the altar,
But my own
Wounded heart.

THE PRICE

Anguish, yes,
But not despair.

This agony that
Ties your breath
Is a law
The fruitful
Must bear.

Ask the
Almost-mother,
Her body
Heaving and torn —
Only from
Exquisite pain
Is beauty born.

DAY-OLD CHILD

My day-old child lay in my arms.
With my lips against his ear
I whispered strongly, "How I wish —
I wish that you could hear;

"I've a hundred wonderful things to say
(A tiny cough and a nod),
Hurry, hurry, hurry and grow
So I can tell you about God."

My day-old baby's mouth was still
And my words only tickled his ear.
But a kind of a light passed through his eyes,
And I saw this thought appear:

"How I wish I had a voice and words;
I've a hundred things to say.
Before I forget I'd tell you of God —
I left Him yesterday."

INVESTMENT

How enviously
I watched
The rose bush
Bear her bud —
Such an easy,
Lovely birth.
And
At that moment
I wished
The sweet myth
Were true —
That I could
Pluck you,
My child,
From some
Green vine.

But now
As you breathe,
Through flesh
That was mine
(Gently in the
Small circle
Of my arms),
I see
The wisdom
Of investment.

The easy gift
Is easy to forget.
But what is bought
With coin of pain—
Is dearly kept.

FROM A WOMAN

Is it, then,
That the trunk
Of the tree
Is man,
And the branch
Is me?

Oh, look—
How high
The leaves lean
To the sky,
And the springtime
Blossoms burst
To beauty,
Then to fruit.

Is there
A wish more worthy
Than to be
A bearer of harvests
Eternally?

GOD SPEAKS
TO ABRAHAM

Why
The almost-sacrifice?
Why the knife
Above your only son
While you wept?

Oh, Abraham,
I needed one
Who could understand.
There will be
Another lifted
On the hill
Of sacrifice.
And another
Father will watch,
Will weep.

But no
Merciful angel,
No man,
Oh, none
Shall stay
Death's hand
To save
My son.

TO MY ANCESTORS

I wonder—
Did I peek
Through the veil
Impatiently,
While you slowly
Forged
The bonds that
Brought me to
Mortality?

And
Do you now stand
Where I stood
Yesterday,
Your cheeks against
Heaven's curtain,
And pray—
Pray fervently
For me to forge
The bonds that
Bring us to
Eternity?

FULL CIRCLE

I shall close the circle, Grandmother,
Whose first half brought
You to these mountains.

On eight-year-steady legs you walked
Beside the wagon, brushing the dust
From your mouth with hands that
In the night reached out for
The dolls you left in Nottingham.
Your wide eyes watched the wooden
Coffin close over your sister Lucy,
A mother's tear frozen on her still face.
Fourteen hundred miles of strange night noises
And the hurt of hunger
And feet that cried for rest.
"But where are we going, Mother?"
"To Zion, dear. Hold the blanket tight."
"Mother, what is Zion?"
"Zion is the pure in heart. Sleep."

Did you know, Grandmother,
As you laid your daughter in a cradle
That she would lay a daughter in a cradle
Who would close the circle?
This bit of lace you brought from
Over the sea will be in my pocket.
And I will pray that you are there
Among the hosts that go before,
Keeping the pillar of fire.

I may have a child who cries out in the night
For his own bed in the valley of the Wasatch.
He won't understand why there are no trains
To travel the fourteen hundred miles.
He may turn to me as we lie on the prairie floor.
"But where are we going, Mother?"
"To build the New Jerusalem.
Hold the blanket tight."
"But why are we going, Mother?"
"Because Christ is there."

Our circle, Grandmother,
And Adam's larger circle, too:
Eden of old,
Jerusalem anew.

TO THE CHRISTIAN
NOW BLESSED WITH
ROSES INSTEAD OF
TAR AND FEATHERS

Remember Aesop's
Tale of the
Traveler?
Please note:
The wind failed
To make him
Shed his coat.
It was the sun
That won.

MONTHLY FAST

One foodless day—
An inspired control:
Good rest
For my body,
Good exercise
For my soul.

WATER AND SPIRIT

My birth today
Is substance of
Heaven's true poetry:

Baptized into
Christ's burial—
God's perfect simile.

THE WATCHERS

There is a tomb
In old Jerusalem
Where one is told
Christ spent
Death's interim.
And many walk
That way
In curiosity.

"Three days
Behind the stone,"
He said,
"And then
A longer time
In heaven before
I come again."

But few
There are
Who watch
That door.

PROVISION FOR THE END

What to do when
The dawn brings night
And the moon spins out
And the stars fall white?

Wait calm in the silence
The black sky spilled:
Your lamp will light—
If it is filled.

JUDGED

I don't fret
As to where
My soul will
Be assigned—
Whether I'll find
Me with the Celestial
Or not quite
Qualify.

It's simple:
Water meets
It's own level—
So shall I.

EARTH-SOUL

The earth
Has a soul—
I know.
How else came
The sorry groans
That heaved
A rush of
Fire and wind
And blood and
Crashing stones?

She felt the
Sad procession
Climb the hill—
She heard
The nails—
She knew.
And with the
Bursting
Of the heart
Upon the cross,
Her heart burst
Too.

GOD SPEAKS

Death is ugly?
Oh, my children,
No.

If you knew
The beauty
That begins where
Your sight fails,
You would run,
Run, run,
And leap
With open arms
Into eternity.

But sad
Is a harvest
Of green wheat.

And,
So you would
Feverishly
Cling to earth
And finish
Your mortal task,
I merely gave
Death
An ugly mask.

OF PLACES FAR

To me Istanbul
Was only a name,
Until a picture
You took
Of the Blue Mosque
Came.

I don't receive
Postcards from heaven
Showing Saint Peter
At prayer,
But, oh—that place
Is real enough,
Now that
You are there.

BOUND

There's something strangely false in our
Assured, complete goodbye,
For love's the blood in the flesh of the soul
And the soul will never die.

So—friendly, fondly, as I may
In God's approving view,
I'll call across eternity
For messages of you.

WOMAN-CHILD

As a child
I saw her hand
(That had guided
My mouth to her breast)
Posed carefully
To rest
Upon a pleated robe.
Unwillingly
It froze.

Will she mind,
I wonder,
That when next we meet
She will not find
A small brown head
For her fingers
To caress,
But instead
A woman-child
In woman's dress?

MEMORIAL

This rose I give
To your grave
Is lovely, yes,
But I must confess
A little shame
To place these petals
Beside your name.

Tomorrow the rose
Is brown and dead,
Now bright and vernal.
But, oh—
Your season
Is eternal.

POINT OF VIEW

Sun and mountain meet.
"Look," I say.
"Sunset!"

But I forget
That far away
An islander
Wipes morning
From his eyes
And watches
The same sun
Rise.

What's birth?
And death?
What's near
Or far?
It all depends
On where you are.

DEATH

Death is the great forget, they said,
A mindless, restful leaving
Of all consciousness and care
In a vast unweaving.

And so I waited, cramped and still,
For approaching Death to bring
Forgetfulness—but all he brought
Was a huge remembering.

MEMENTOS
OF MORTALITY

I do not write
That my words
Might save
Some small
Piece of me
Beyond the grave.
Oh, I shall
Be quick long
Past the day
The last reader
Has put the
Book away.
And with use
Fulfilled,
These words
I write shall be
Happy mementos
Of mortality.